To Sharon!

Merry Christmas 2015!

From one foodie to another.
Happy cooking. Hope you
come to love the recipies and
will share them often with
family and friends.

Bon Appétit
Carline Bergstrom

DEDICATION

To treasured moments together in the kitchen creating and partaking in good eats with my mom, siblings, husband, extended family and friends.

In loving memory of my husband
Lars Johan Georg Bengtsson

TABLE OF CONTENTS

ABOUT THE AUTHOR

Carline Bengtsson began her "mosaic" life in Jamaica where she was born. While still a young girl, she departed Jamaica for St. Paul, Minnesota in the summer of 1973. She completed her formative schooling at St. Agnes Catholic School, and went on to study business and art on the Lutheran campus of Concordia College St. Paul (now Concordia University), graduating in 1986. She has earned a Mini MBA from the University of St. Thomas in 1990 and a Marketing Certificate from the University of Pennsylvania Wharton Executive Education in 2006. Carline has a successful career at the world's leading medical technology company, Medtronic, Inc. and throughout her career at Medtronic she has also had the opportunity to work and live in Switzerland. Prior to joining Medtronic, she also worked for Honeywell and Blue Cross and Blue Shield of MN. Carline is an engaged community volunteer, serving on several boards: St. Paul's East Side Arts Council, the American Swedish Institute and the St. Paul Schubert Club.

Although her education was grounded in the Catholic and Lutheran faiths, Carline grew up in the Covenant church where she cultivated her Scandinavian roots through her faith, love of music and shared Swedish traditions. In 1988, a chance meeting on a boat outing brought Carline together with her husband-to-be, Lars Johan Georg Bengtsson, born and raised in Sweden, but now at home in Minnesota. Carline and Lars married in the fall of 1994 and resided for fifteen years in downtown St. Paul with a panoramic view of the waters of the Mississippi River on which they first met. They traveled the world, but always returned to Sweden for summers and Christmases.

Carline spent quiet time immersing herself in Swedish language, culture and traditional music. Her love of singing led her to be part of the formation of a popular and well respected Scandinavian a-cappella quintet, "Flickorna Fem". The group has performed throughout the Midwest, toured Sweden and performed for Their Majesties, The King and Queen of Sweden, including Benny Andersson formerly of the singing sensation ABBA, during their visits to the American Swedish Institute in Minneapolis. Carline is described by her family and friends as a medical device industry specialist, a sports enthusiast, passionate soprano, biker chick, fashion and interior design diva, hostess supreme, and connoisseur AND chef of enticing and deliriously delicious eats.

FOREWORD

Having known Carline and her wonderful family for many years, when asked to tryout her recipes, I was happy to oblige. Being a chef, I am often asked for tips of the trade, yet many are intimidated to cook for me and few send their personal recipes my way. I love the confidence and flare for which Carline boldly presents her recipes to me and the passion for which she speaks of this endeavor. For me, those two qualities are the first measure of a chef. Obviously, you must have some talent and a palette. Carline has always been a foodie; she is fully engaged in every dish! When she visits my restaurants, serving her a dish is an adventure in and of itself! She has a passion for food and a curiosity about each dish that drives her to perfection when creating her own recipes. I have known that she has the palette and flare but honestly, when trying these recipes, I am amazed at their simple elegance. Even though classic by some measure, Carline has an incredibly innovative take on them.

Again, pleasantly surprised with the wine pairings, from one professional to another, I commend Carline. The current trend of Local, Organic and Sustainable cooking is how I grew up. The connection that Carline makes with these principles tells me that it is in her DNA as well. The wines and the pairings are superb and the fact that they are from a local vineyard indicates her commitment to her environment large and small. She shows the experience beyond her years in the kitchen. From the poached pears to the scallops these recipes will stand the test of time and are not only creative but can be addictive. A great addition to any collection, these recipes are a wonderful addition to any event whether a large soiree or an intimate dinner with friends. Enjoy!

-David Fhima

INTRODUCTION

I have had the great blessing to live a culturally rich "mosaic" life that have given me the opportunity to enjoy culinary inspirations from Jamaica to Sweden, Asia and in between. The passion for food preparation and presentation was grounded in me through the combination of all my "home countries", Jamaica, Sweden and the US. This book is a testimony to my food journeys and for all the love and support from my husband Lars and my dear family and friends that have been guests at my dinner table. Their encouragement helped me realize this book. It has been a fantastic creative journey and my wish is that you will be as satisfied enjoying my recipes at your dinner tables as I have been in creating and sharing them. I hope that your taste buds will be infused with a "mosaic" of wonderful smells and tastes through continents, cultures, and food menus to enjoy and be inspired by. Be inspired by a mosaic of spices and food ingredients prepared and combined in ways to tease your taste buds and leave you guessing the roots of each food creation presented.

My story is about my Jamaican roots morphing into Scandinavian life, inspired by travels throughout the world which all influenced the birth of my "mosaic" inspired cooking. The journey began with introduction to the Jamaican cooking tradition that uses a mix of customary and other blends of ingredients like nutmeg, curry, jerk, coconut milk, ginger, hard dough bread, scallions and black pepper seasonings as the basis for daily meals. From my Swedish food tradition I have the daily use of dill, leak, potatoes, crisp bread and white pepper with great sauces to all meals adding the perfect balance between mild and spicy and plenty and sparse. A potpourri of spices from my Jamaican roots, Swedish and Asian cooking can be found in my kitchen as well as plenty of simple, nutritious ingredients like spinach, cilantro, mint, parsley, tomatoes, cucumbers, mixed greens, avocado, sprouts…and more.

You might wonder now, how does a little girl from Jamaica grow up to be Swedish in the US with an affinity to all these food cultures? For me the path was carved out with my mother's desire for a better life in a new world called the USA or "foreign" (as it is fondly referred to by Jamaicans). We moved to the state of Minnesota, where in the 1970's it was almost impossible to maintain "Jamaican-ness" in a state filled with "Swedish-ness". Becoming Minnesotan meant an immersion into the Scandinavian culture either willingly or through osmosis. However, home was where Jamaican traditions were maintained through daily cooking and weekly Sunday afternoon family dinners around the kitchen table. As a young girl I would watch my mother prepare meals in the kitchen, sometimes even providing her a helping hand. My passion for cooking didn't come to light until several years later. Eating a good home-cooked meal was something I liked and not much more than that. I always imagined that my artistic ability would lead me into the gallery space, providing unknown artists a venue for showing their work.

Instead, I started using the dinner table as my own canvas and the food became my paint pallet and choice of expression.

My Swedish culture was already well established for me as a Minnesotan, but when I met my Swedish husband Lars it blossomed with his guidance and introduction to all things Swedish. Lars Bengtsson, from Sweden, who made Minnesota home, came into my life unexpectedly through a chance meeting by a mutual friend. Over the course of our relationship and subsequent marriage, Lars introduced me to what I would have considered unusual culturally infused Scandinavian, Southern European and Asian foods at home and throughout our travels. I, on the other hand, made sure he was further culturally blessed with Jamaican foodie traditions. He was my companion when I, for the first time after leaving Jamaica as a young girl two decades earlier, revisited the land of my birth to reconnect with my roots and extended family, spring of 1994.

My very first visit back to Jamaica brought back all the smells, tastes of food and memories dating back to my youth. Lars confirmed, as I through his eyes also could see, the beauty of the Jamaican culture, people and land that I instantly felt connected to again. Our island road trip took us to Ocho Rios, Mavis Bank-St. Andrews, Kingston, Montego Bay and Negril. At every destination we would enjoy points of interest, great food and drinks. Jamaican breakfast consisted of Ackee (The Jamaican National Fruit) and Salt Fish with fried plantains and hard-dough bread; for lunch a variety of meals such as Jamaican patties or jerk chicken. Dinners featured fresh fish, curried chicken or curried goat with rice and peas ....and to that great Red Stripe Beer and late evenings Jamaican rum was a must.

We visited many places and met many of my relatives, collecting new exciting experiences, one of them being driving the wicked, traitorous Jamaican roads as we enjoyed the beautiful scenery of the island and the Caribbean Sea with a view as far and wide as the eyes could capture. If one wants to experience life on the edge coupled with near death, just get behind the wheel of a car in Jamaica and drive. Navigating the narrow roads is an intense proposition not meant for mere mortals with vehicles, pedestrians, and animals sharing the same space the size of a single lane of traffic. The effort was so worth it and the roads were never a challenge for Lars as he like a true Jamaican repeated, "no problem mon." Along the way we passed children walking to school in their nicely pressed uniforms. Memories of years gone by came rushing back to me when I would walk the main thorough fair of South Camp Road to Kingston's Alpha Kinda Prep School each morning. The day would begin with a bowl of malt-o-meal oatmeal or an egg and toast for breakfast. I would then get dressed into my school uniform; grab my schoolbooks and head out the front door to begin the long walk towards South Camp Road to the open classroom setting surrounded by flower gardens flanked with pear, avocado, mango and banana trees. I do remember always being on my best behavior because the teachers, sisters dressed in white, were not afraid to provide a bit of discipline with their rulers.

Both my parents were from families of twelve siblings, of which they were the youngest. So I essentially had twenty-two aunts and uncles plus countless first cousins I could visit. We visited my first cousins, Carmen and Michael, who lived in Kingston. At her home I met my second cousins, her three daughters who were very welcoming and excited to meet their cousin from "foreign." For them it was a surprise that I didn't sound Jamaican to them! They wondered what happened to my accent, to which I explained that moving away as a child played a role in the development of my new dialect, which was now a combination of Jamaican, Minnesotan and Scandinavian, specifically Swedish. Carmen prepared some great home cooking for us which consisted of boiled bananas, yam, dumpling and beef stew.

We all decided to drive to my family's old home where the life I once knew as a native Jamaican ended for me as I embarked to a new way of life in the states. Along the way Carmen would yell out the car window "irie mon" to everyone she knew. I recognized right away when we came upon the old neighborhood that the grocery store was no longer in business. How sad, I thought. This once vibrant corner grocery was now boarded up. This is where I once came to buy chewing gum, lollypops and tamarind rolled in brown sugar.

Upon entering the gates of my former home at "1A Woodford Crescent" we were greeted by the family who was now living there; they graciously let us enter their home for some reminiscing in a place which held so many childhood memories. I was taken back in time; from the yard outside and the veranda in the front of the house, to the rooms inside the house, and the tree I once climbed as a child, keeping up with the boys, was now only a trunk. I remembered it all vividly well.

We continued with Carmen and Michael to the Blue Mountains to visit my aunt and uncle and their pig farm with over three hundred pigs. Farming was the way of life for my aunt and uncle and the cousins who were still living at home. Their whole family pitched in to help grow vegetables, fruits, flowers and raise pigs. Each Friday their truck is loaded up to make the drive to Kingston Farmer's Market. Aunt Ethlyn reminded me a lot of my maternal grandmother Jane. She couldn't believe that it was me she was looking at as I stood before her after so many years. Both she and Carmen reminded me of how shy I was as a child and also didn't hesitate to comment on how much weight I had gained from my meager beginnings. This made Lars chuckle because he always referred to me as "Flamingo Legs" so, I'm sure he couldn't imagine how I could have been much skinnier. We all laughed at the thought as we stood in the cool crisp outdoor air with no denying that we were on a pig farm. Bully beef and hard-dough bread was our lunch for the day. I almost forgot how good it tasted. Even though I spent a short time with the family a lifetime of memories remained with us all.

We left my relatives and continued our trip to different "must see" destinations and enjoyed food at great restaurants. A dinner to remember was at the Almond Tree Restaurant with a view of the sea while we ate callaloo, potato and yam with red snapper and beef tenderloin. Food tastes of long ago never escaped my taste buds or my sense of smell. It was as I had always remembered eating callaloo greens and yam. It's like remembering the taste of spinach as it hits your mouth or even delectable chocolate covered strawberries.

I truly enjoyed our visits to the General Food Market at Ocean Village Center where I bought canned cod fish in salt water to go with the canned Ackee that would make their way back home to Minnesota for a future breakfast. Just walking through the market I saw the things I once ate as a child: fresh sugar cain, fresh coconut, mangoes, avocados, plantains, yams, callaloo, tamarind in the shell or rolled in brown sugar. A rush of the unique flavors penetrated my sense of taste, taking them in all at once, but yet pinpointing each flavor individually as my taste buds recalled each one.

This trip brought so many memories that helped ground me and also show me the bases for my culinary interests and curiosity.

Lars and I returned to Jamaica within the same year. This time for our wedding! Everything I had just experienced seven months earlier was now shared with our wedding guest of family and friends that joined us from all corners of the US, Sweden, The Bahamas and of course Jamaica. We repeated our travels to Ocho Rios, Montego Bay and Negril. Equally delightful the second time around, for now my life had come full circle.

We returned to Minnesota and the Scandinavian traditions imparted on me. Now married to a Swede the dinner preparation discussion was always around if we should have potatoes or rice. He grew up with potatoes at the dinner table and I, with rice. In some ways learning to speak Swedish was less painful than giving in to eating potatoes once again instead of rice. Thank goodness our travels to southern Europe and Asia introduced another option called noodles. We were always true to our food roots but were never shy to introduce something new into our regiment of mostly potatoes and sometimes rice. I also became partial to steak seasoning, yes steak seasoning. It's not just for steak as you will come to see when trying the recipes on the forthcoming pages. The Scandinavian favorite, dill, is also a staple in my food creations together with mint and cilantro. Spices are meant to be experienced in out of the ordinary ways. Take a leap to cook with your heart, knowing that it's absolutely OK to let your taste buds explore finding the right balance between just enough (like Swedes would say: "lagom") and really good ("jättegott").

As the years went by we shared dinners with family and friends and my interest in the kitchen became a passion, always seeking out unique ways to craft and present a new dish. At the end of the day our bodies are nourished and lives enriched by the foods we love to eat; by our interest in going out on a limb to try a new, out of the ordinary dish whether it is at home, out on the town or wherever our travels take us throughout the world.

The richness life has to offer can sometimes be found at the end of your fork and in that bottle just un-corked. This book is written as a lasting legacy to my beloved husband, family and friends who have always encouraged me to dream big like the Chinese fortune states – "In dreams and in life, nothing is impossible."

"**L**ive well – **O**pen your heart – **V**isibly shine – **E**njoy each day!"

Carline Bengtsson

First Course

Seafood Avocado

Salad Endive

Pear Salad

Stacked Feta

Capri Karen

Ingredients

3 Firmly ripe medium size avocados
24 Large pre-cooked shrimp or
3 Cups crayfish tails dill flavored
3 Tea spoons chopped fresh dill
¾ Cup extra virgin olive oil
1 Table spoon dried dill weed
1 Table spoon lemon juice
½ Tea spoon black pepper

Salt to taste

Avocados are natures best and go great with everything. When selecting avocados they should respond to slight pressure from your thumb but still firm to the touch. With 3 firmly ripe medium size avocados selected, slice them in half and carefully remove the seeds. Place the 6 avocado halves on separate serving plates. If they tilt downward on the plate, with a knife remove a small piece of the skin underneath, this will allow the avocado to lay on the plate more horizontal. To the center of each avocado add your preferred seafood selection: 4 large pre-cooked shrimp or ½ cup crayfish tails (pictured), dill flavored. In a measuring cup add ¾ cup extra virgin olive oil, 1 table spoon dried dill weed, 1 table spoon lemon juice, ½ tea spoon black pepper and salt to taste. Vigorously stir, and then drizzle 2-3 table spoons over each Seafood Avocado plate. Top off by sprinkling a ½ teaspoon chopped fresh dill over each plate and whallah! This tropical fruit should be combined with Winehaven's own tropical fruit blend, Frontenac Gris.

SEAFOOD AVOCADO

Prepare the day of, one hour before serving

Serves: 6

"A ripe-to-the-minute avocado is halved and filled with…., cool pink baby shrimp, and a spray of dill is more than the sum of its parts."

Nina – St. Paul, MN

SALAD ENDIVE

Prepare the day of, one hour before serving
Serves: 6

Already have bacon on the menu for breakfast? Steak up some extra for this divine Salad Endive. The bacon can be prepared the day before crumbled and refrigerated, ready to be added to the salad the day of your dinner party. This salad is beautiful and equally delightfully tasty, making it a good compliment to any wine. However, may I suggest Winehaven's Lakeside Red? You will not be disappointed. With ingredients ready to be combined, start by placing a healthy portion of salad mix on six individual plates. To each plate add 2 table spoons of crumbled goat cheese; 1-1 ½ table spoon of crumbled gorgonzola; 1-1 ½ table spoon crumbled bacon and 1 ½ table spoon crumbled honey roasted pecans. Remove stems from mission figs; halve three each per plate. In measuring cup add ¼ cup extra virgin olive oil and ¾ cup fig balsamic vinegar. Stir vigorously and drizzle 2 to 3 table spoons over each salad right before serving. Bon Appétit!

Ingredients

2 Bags of salad spring mix -
    baby lettuces, greens & radicchio
1 Cup crumbled goat cheese
1 Cup crumbled gorgonzola
1 Cup crumbled bacon
1 Bag mission figs dried fruit
2/3 Cup crumbled honey roasted pecans
¾ Cup fig balsamic vinegar
¼ Cup extra virgin olive oil

"*Of all the salads I have had this was by far my favorite; very good blend of tastes.*"
Todd – Lino Lakes, MN

Pear Salad

Prepare just before serving
Serves: 6

Ingredients

3 Firm ripe Bose Pears
1 Bag salad spring mix
1 Bag arugula
6 Table spoons crumbled blue cheese
6 Table spoons honey roasted pecans
6 Table spoons dried cranberries
6 Fluid ounce Balsamic Vinaigrette Salad dressing

Begin by placing ½ cup combined spring mix and arugula to 6 salad plates. Slice the Bose Pears in half horizontally; remove seeds from the center of each pear and place one halved pear in the center of each salad plate. Sprinkle 1 table spoon each blue cheese Gorgonzola, cranberries and honey roasted pecans on each salad plate.

Drizzle 2 table spoons of balsamic vinaigrette salad dressing over each salad just before serving. Start this first course with Winehaven's Riesling.

"Carline's artful food is always a treat for guests as it is visually wonderful and deliciously prepared. She is very talented as a chef and always pairs the food with just the right wine."
Sarah – St. Paul, MN

Stacked Feta

Prepare just before serving
Serves: 4

Ingredients

5 Ounce Package baby arugula
8 Ounce Package chunk feta cheese (produces 8 slices)
2 Large vine tomatoes (produces 6 slices per tomato)
2 Large Cucumbers (8 inches in length and 2 inches in width)
5 Ounce Package alfalfa sprouts
6 Fluid ounce Balsamic Vinaigrette Salad dressing

Simple ingredients elegantly featured for a fantastic first course is the aim of this recipe. Now that all ingredients are in place, first begin by cutting ~1 ½ inches off each end of the cucumbers so that the seeds are visible. Next peel away the cucumber's skin with a potato peeler. Wash the cucumbers and pat dry with paper towels. Now, on a bread board cut the cucumbers in half, so that there are now four halved cucumbers. Stand each half cucumber horizontally and trim each side of the cucumber, removing a sliver. This will allow the cucumbers to lie on their side for ease of stacking. Follow that up with slicing horizontally four (4) ½ inch thick slices for a total of sixteen (16) ½ inch thick cucumber slices.

Same with the tomatoes wash and pat dry with paper towels. Remove a sliver from the top of each tomato and then slice the tomatoes for a total of twelve (12) ½ inch thick tomato slices.

Open the chunk feta cheese package and drain excess liquid. Slicing the long way, produce eight (8) ½ inch thick slices.

Now the fun begins! Stacking order of this salad will be two (2) layers of arugula, cucumber, tomato, feta cheese. End the layering with a slice of cucumber and tomato. Just before serving, drizzle balsamic vinaigrette dressing over the stacked feta salad; top off each salad with a pinch of alfalfa sprouts. Feast on this salad with Winehaven's Riesling. Cheers to fresh goodness!

"It's a joy to see what she's going to prepare because it's always something different and, perhaps most importantly, we know we will

"Carline has a wonderful way of combining flavors, textures, and colors to create a vividly memorable culinary experience."
Janet – Stillwater, MN

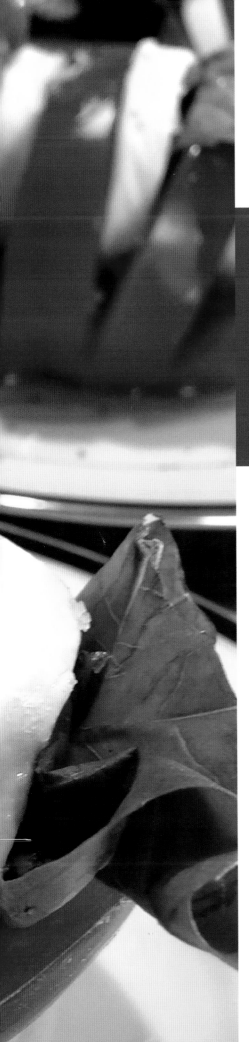

Capri Karen

Prepare just before serving
Serves: 6

Ingredients

6 Vine tomatoes
2 – 8 Ounce Packages fresh Mozzarella
(sliced and ready to serve)
1 – 0.75 Ounce Package fresh basil
¼ Cup extra virgin olive oil
Pinch sea salt
Pinch black pepper

Now that you have picked out 6 nice firm and exceptionally red in color vine tomatoes, it's time to prepare this effortless but tasty salad, Capri Karen. Tomatoes should be at room temperature for best flavor. Place the tomatoes on 6 individual salad plates.

Make four evenly spaced slices in each tomato approximately ¾ of the way down. Next place 1 fresh mozzarella in-between each sliced opening, then repeat the process by adding fresh basil into each sliced opening.

Finish up this salad by drizzling 2 table spoons extra virgin olive oil over each salad followed with sprinklings of sea salt and black pepper over each Capri Karen. Compliment this refreshing salad with Winehaven's Lakeside Chardonnay.

Second Course

Dill Chicken

Lars' Crab Salad

Chicken Noodle Soup

Lemon Ginger Chicken Stir Fry

Beef Szechuan Stir Fry

Filet BBQ on a Bed of Asparagus

Dill Chicken

Prepare the day of
Serves: 6

"Dining at Carline's table is warm and inviting. Her cooking is exemplarily: well prepared, tastefully done, and presented with an artistic flare."
Edna & Larry – Maple Grove, MN

Ingredients

6 Boneless Chicken breast filets	18 Small New Red potatoes
4 Cups water	2 Stalks fresh dill
¼ Cup extra virgin olive oil	18 Asparagus
2 Table spoons dried dill weed seasoning	2 Firmly ripe avocados
2 Table spoons steak seasoning	1 Package alfalfa sprouts
1 Table spoon finely chopped garlic	1 Tea spoon lime juice

Time to prepare the three main ingredients: Chicken, Potatoes and Asparagus. First butterfly each chicken breast, slicing them horizontally in half before placing in large skillet. Halve each potato and place in a deep pot. Fill pot with water until water line just hits the top of the potatoes; add 2 stalks fresh dill, cover and place on burner. Wash asparagus and evenly cut away the thicker portion of each spear. Place in a large skillet, drizzle with extra virgin olive oil and add ½ cup water. Let stand until later for sautéing.

Let's not forget about the avocado. Slice each avocado in half, removing the seed. Quarter each halved avocado and peel away the skin; place in plastic container and drizzle 1 tea spoon lime juice over the sliced avocados. Cover and place in fridge to keep cool.

Start the potatoes under medium to high heat setting, bringing to a boil and then lower the burner to low to medium heat setting. Set timer to seventeen (17) minutes. Check the potatoes with a potato tester after 10-12 minutes. If little to no resistance, the potatoes are ready, otherwise cook for a few more minutes, checking frequently. Remove directly from the heat and drain off liquid. Place paper towels over the potatoes and re-cover. This will keep them moist until time to serve up.

While the potatoes are cooking pour the remaining 3 ½ cups water over chicken breasts in large skillet; add ¼ cup extra virgin olive oil, 2 table spoons each dried dill weed and steak seasoning and 1 table spoon finely chopped garlic. Place cover over skillet and bring contents to a boil over medium heat. Keep covered and continue to simmer over medium to low heat setting for 30 minutes; turn chicken frequently until cooked all the way through, and tender to the touch. Keep covered at lowest setting, allowing the chicken breasts to slowly simmer and soak in the juices.

Bring skillet with asparagus to a boil under medium-high heat for thirty to forty-five seconds; remove directly from heat and drain liquid. The asparagus should be al dente, firm but crisp. On 6 large serving plates place 6 asparagus stacked in the center of the plate; next add 6 halved potatoes to each plate to one side of the asparagus. Place two pieces of tender chicken breast filets to the other side of the asparagus. Add a generous amount of sauce to each plate. Top off the chicken with 1-3 slices of avocado and a pinch of alfalfa sprouts.

Welcome your guest to the table with this beautiful and equally tasty meal, enhancing the flavors with Winehaven's Gewürztraminer.

"*Each ingredient complements the next and heightens the flavor experience.*"

Matt – Maple Grove, MN

Lars' Crab Salad

Prepare the day of | Serves: 6

Ingredients
3 Packages, 6 Ounces
　　each fresh crab meat
6 Large eggs
2 Bags of salad spring mix
18 Red grape tomatoes
6 Tea spoons capers
3 Table spoons caviar
¾ Cup extra virgin olive oil
1 Table spoon dried dill weed
1 Table spoon lemon juice
½ Tea spoon black pepper
Salt to taste

How do you like your yolk?

Soft – cook 6-8 minutes
Medium – cook 10-12 minutes
Hard – cook 12-14 minutes

Yum I say to fresh crab! But before you can begin to enjoy every bite of Lars' Crab Salad, eggs cooked to perfection your way is a must. When the 6 eggs are ready; peel away the egg shell and slice in half and set off to the side on a platter for later. In a measuring cup add ¾ cup extra virgin olive oil, 1 table spoon dried dill weed, 1 table spoon lemon juice, ½ tea spoon black pepper and salt to taste.

Next, on 6 individual plates place a healthy portion of the spring salad mix. Slice horizontally 3 each red grape tomatoes and place around the outer perimeter of each plate. Top the spring mix on each plate with ½ cup each crab meat. To each plate add 2 halved egg to the top of the crab meat; sprinkle with 1 tea spoon capers; top the egg with ½ tea spoon caviar. Vigorously stir the extra virgin olive oil with the already added ingredients in the measuring cup and then drizzle 2-3 table spoons over each salad plate.

At the table add cracked black pepper and salt as desired to taste. Now before you dig in to enjoy, its best I say Varsågod (you may begin) and Skål (cheers) to Lars' Crab Salad with Winehaven's La Crescent.

Chicken Noodle Soup

Prepare and serve the day of or freeze, unthaw, slowly heat up; serve and enjoy
Serves: 6 -8

Ingredients

12 Cups water
1 Package 1.75 Pounds boneless, skinless chicken thighs
2 Cubes chicken bouillon
2-3 Ounces spaghetti noodles
3 Table spoons steak seasoning
¼ Cup extra virgin olive oil
1 Cup combined sliced yellow and red mini sweet peppers
2 Cups sweet thinly cut carrots
½ Cup chopped sugar snap peas
2 Cups packed fresh baby spinach

In a large covered soup pot add 12 cups water and 1.75 pounds boneless, skinless chicken thighs. Cover pot and bring pot to a boil over medium heat, cooking for 10 minutes until chicken is cooked all the way through. Remove the chicken thighs from the pot and place on a cutting board, slicing each into smaller pieces and then adding them back into the soup pot.

To the pot add 2 cubes chicken bouillon, 2-3 ounces spaghetti noodles, 3 table spoons steak seasoning and ¼ cup extra virgin olive oil. Depending on the depth of your soup pot, the noodles may need to be broken in half. Bring contents to a boil over medium heat and simmer for 2-3 minutes until noodles are just soft to the touch, however not mushy.

Turn heat source to between medium and low setting then add remaining ingredients: 2 cups sweet thinly cut carrots; ½ cup chopped sugar snap peas and 2 cups packed fresh baby spinach. Stir until spinach is just wilted. Remove from heat source and dish up, adding 1 ½ cup soup to each soup bowl.

Chicken noodle soup is always inviting; always a palette pleaser. To chicken noodle, there is no better combination than Winehaven's Lakeside Chardonnay.

"Good, simple flavors that stand out whether it's soup, salad or an entrée."
Patti – Spring Park, MN

"Carline's recipes are very tasty and I love the combinations she uses for each dish."
Robin – Lakeville, MN

Lemon Ginger Chicken Stir Fry

Prepare day of
Serves 4

Ingredients

1 Package 1.25 pounds boneless, skinless chicken breast
1 ½ Cup lemon ginger sesame dressing
1/3 Cup extra virgin olive oil
1 Table spoon minced garlic
1 Table spoon steak seasoning
1 Cup finely chopped red and yellow mini sweet peppers
2 Cups chopped fresh green beans or sugar snap peas
¾ Cup chopped mint leaves
¾ Cup chopped cilantro or parsley
4 scallions trimmed and sliced at an angle into pieced

The use of flavorful salad dressings is another one of my favorite ingredients to use in food preparation. For this meal the staple dressing is lemon ginger sesame with just the right flavors to complement this chicken stir fry dish to be served over your choice of either rice or noodles. To prepare this meal, first cut the chicken breast into small pieces and place into a large covered steak pan.

Add to the chicken 1/3 cup extra virgin olive oil, 1 table spoon minced garlic and 1 table spoon steak seasoning. Cover the chicken and sauté over medium heat for 10 minutes, turning frequently. After 7 minutes turn heat setting to low and continue to sauté for the final 3 minutes. Pour 1 ½ cup lemon ginger sesame dressing over the chicken and bring to a simmer over medium heat.

Add 2 cups chopped fresh beans or sugar snap peas. After 30 seconds add the remaining ingredients: 1 cup finely chopped red and yellow mini sweet peppers; ¾ cup chopped mint leaves; ¾ cup chopped cilantro or parsley and 4 scallions trimmed and sliced at an angle into pieces. Blend ingredients together and immediately remove from the stove. Pour in a large bowl and serve at the table family style over rice or noodles. Cheers to stir fry with Winehaven's Frontenac Gris.

No matter if its breakfast, lunch, or dinner, Carline's meals are consistently presented with exquisite perfection. It's a joy to see what she's going to prepare because it's always something different."
Michael & Ryoko – Tokyo, Japan

Beef Szechuan Stir Fry

Prepare the day of
Serves: 2-4

Ingredients

1 Pound Stew beef
1 Cup water
4 Table spoons extra virgin olive oil
2 Tea spoons minced garlic
1 ½ Table spoons steak seasoning
1 Cup chopped asparagus

1 Cup chopped red bell pepper
1 Cup chopped sugar snap peas
1 Cup chopped cilantro
1 Cup classic stir fry sauce
1 ½ Tea spoons Szechuan spicy stir fry sauce

In a large covered skillet combine 1 pound stew beef, 1 cup water, 4 table spoons extra virgin olive oil, 2 tea spoons minced garlic, 1½ table spoons steak seasoning, 1 cup classic stir fry sauce and 1 ½ tea spoons Szechuan spicy stir fry sauce.

Cover and cook over medium heat for 15-20 minutes, stirring frequently, until meat is done. Add 1 cup chopped asparagus and bring to a boil for not more than 30 seconds.

Finally add the remaining three ingredients – 1 cup chopped sugar snap peas, 1 cup chopped red bell pepper and 1 cup chopped cilantro. Stir for 10 seconds; remove from the heat source and serve over either rice or noodles. Pair this cuisine with Winehaven's Gewürztraminer.

"*Carline has a knack for presenting dishes which combine cutting-edge elegance with light, unfussy flavors grounded in the freshest of ingredients. She seems to effortlessly array colors and ingredients with results that make each diner feel a part of the creative process.*"
Nina – St. Paul, MN

Filet BBQ on a Bed of Asparagus

Prepare the day of - Serves: 6

Ingredients

3 Packages – 1.35 pounds per package containing two each filet Minong
¾ Cup BBQ Sauce
5 Table spoons extra virgin olive oil
3 Tea spoons butter

2 Table spoons steak seasoning
1 Table spoon freshly chopped rosemary (1-2 sprigs)
18 Asparagus
½ Cup water
1 – 15 ounces can whole beets
1 – 14 ounces can quartered artichoke hearts

First thing, first open each can of artichoke and beets; drain liquid. Remove residual liquid from quartered artichokes by patting dry with paper towels and place in a bowl off to the side. Next, quarter each whole beets and also place in a bowl off to the side. Wash asparagus and evenly cut away the thicker portion of each spear. Place in a large skillet, drizzle with extra virgin olive oil and add ½ cup water. Let stand until later for sautéing. Now on to the filets - In a large cast iron covered skillet place the six filets; add ¾ cup BBQ sauce, 4 table spoons extra virgin olive oil, top each filet with a ½ tea spoon butter and sprinkle over each filet 2 table spoons steak seasoning. Prepare the rosemary by holding your finger at the top of the sprig and running your finger down in the opposite direction of the way the rosemary needles grow, collecting 1 table spoon. Chop the rosemary and add to the skillet with other ingredients.

Cover skillet and over medium heat simmer the filets, turning frequently until desired wellness[1] is achieved with use of a temperature gauge. When the filets are finished remove immediately from skillet; place on a platter and cover with foil to keep warm. Take quartered artichokes and add to sauce in cast iron skillet from the filet preparation. Bring the sauce and artichokes to a simmer for not more than one minute; then turn down to lowest temperature.   In a small sauce pan add the quartered beets and remaining 1 table spoon extra virgin olive oil. Sauté the beets over medium heat for not more than one minute, then turn off heat source. Bring skillet with asparagus to a boil under medium-high heat for thirty to forty-five seconds; remove directly from heat and drain liquid. The asparagus should be al dente, firm but crisp. On 6 large serving plates place 6 asparagus side by side; add filet on top of the bed of asparagus and top off each filet with quartered artichokes and beets evenly (about 5-6 each); let them fall where they may. Add BBQ sauce on the side in a single sauce holder and serve immediately. Be prepared to take your taste buds to new heights. Don't forget to pour Winehaven's Dear Garden Red Chisago. Cheers!

[1] Rare - 140°F; Medium Rare - 145°F; Medium - 160°F; Medium well - 165°F; Well - 170°F

Third Course

Poached Pears

Raspberry Cream

Swedish Crepes

Fig Delight

Poached Pears

Prepare the day before
Serves: 4

Ingredients

4 Firm Bose Pears with stem
4 Mint leaves with stem
3 Bottles Winehaven Riesling (6 ½ cups)
2 Cinnamon sticks
16 Ounces pure dark brown sugar

Peel pears with potato peeler leaving stem in place – may need to shave a little from the base of the pear to ensure posture on serving plate will be upright. Place peeled pears in medium to large sauce pan and add ingredients; wine, dark brown sugar and cinnamon sticks.

Bring contents to a boil; reduce heat and simmer, checking pears frequently with a potato tester for tenderness. Pears should stay firm, making sure not to overcook. Pear is ready when able to pierce the pear through to the other side. Remove from heat and set in a cool spot to soak overnight. Rotate in sauce as needed for all over color.

Prior to serving, reduce 1/3 of a cup of the sauce over high heat; gently remove the pears by their stem and place on individual serving plates. Garnish with mint; add a scoop of ice-cream; drizzle reduced sauce over each pear; add chocolate syrup to plate as desired and serve.

"The desert was a real treat; the poached pear and ice cream was out of this world. I still carry a picture of this on my phone to share. We had a wonderful dining experience as good as it gets right down to the sparkling water!"

Mike & Debbie – Forest Lake, MN

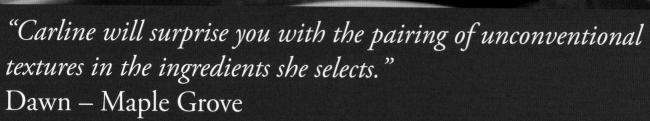

"Carline will surprise you with the pairing of unconventional textures in the ingredients she selects."
Dawn – Maple Grove

Raspberry Cream

Prepare just before serving
Serves: 6

Ingredients

1.75 Quarts size box of Ice cream,
New York Vanilla flavor
6 Ounce package Raspberries
8 Ounce package Pomegranate Seeds
½ Cup dried cranberries
16 Fluid Ounce French Vanilla coffee creamer
1 Pint heavy whipping cream
Syrup chocolate flavor
6 Mint leaves

Take dessert to a whole new level with Raspberry Cream. It's more than the raspberries that makes this a palette pleaser; it's the combination of the sum of the all the ingredients that takes this ice-cream treat to a new level. I would not be offended if you decided to start your meal with dessert first and especially Raspberry Cream.

Begin by adding two scoops of ice cream to 6 each medium size bowls. In each bowl pour 1/8 cup heavy whipping cream, followed up with a 1/8 cup of French vanilla coffee creamer over the scoops of ice-cream.

Next add 4-5 raspberries and a 1 tea spoon each pomegranate seeds and dried cranberries to each bowl. Finally, drizzle over each dessert chocolate flavor syrup, garnish with the mint leaves and sit down to this tempting treat with Winehaven's Raspberry Wine.

"She cooks delicious traditional Swedish dishes… 'Thank you Carline for making me discover many unknown dishes."
Noemie – Paris, France

Swedish Crepes

Prepare just before serving
Serves: 4

Ingredients

3 Eggs
2 ½ Cups milk
1 Cup Flour
Pinch of sugar
Pinch of salt
Butter
Fresh berries
Powdered sugar
Clover honey

Bring together in a mixing bowl the 1 cup flour and half of the milk; using a hand held blender, mix well until the flour is free of clumps. Add in the rest of the milk, 3 eggs, and a pinch of sugar and salt. Mix well to combine all ingredients. Please note that ¼ cup batter will make 2 omelet size crepes.

Under medium heat using an 8" omelet skillet, melt a slice of butter. Starting from the perimeter of the omelet skillet slowly pour 1/8 of a cup of batter around the skillet and inward toward the center of the skillet in a rotating fashion. Set timer to 3 minutes, browning the first side of the crepe for not more than 90 seconds or when there is visible browning and the edge begins to crisp up. Lift the crepe with your finger to introduce the spatula, sliding it towards the center of the crepe. Flip the crepe and brown for the last 90 or so seconds. When ready slide the crepe from the skillet unto a large plate or platter to begin stacking. Repeat the process until a total sixteen (16) thinly lightly browned crepes are prepared.

Just before serving roll up individually four (4) crepes and stack them two by two. Add your favorite fresh berries. Pictured here are blueberries, blackberries and raspberries. Sprinkle with a dusting of powdered sugar and in a circular motion line the edge of the plate with clover honey.

There are two Winehaven selections to choose from. You can't go wrong with Stinger Mead which boasts a spectacular perfume of honey or the Raspberry Wine which is loaded with raspberry flavor.

Fig Delight

Prepare just before serving
Serves: 6

Ingredients

6 Thick diagonal slices of French bread
1 Stick salted butter
4 Ounce package mild goat cheese
6 Tea spoons fig spread
6 Mission figs
6 Mint leaves with stems

Butter both sides of the 6 French bread with the salted butter and place in a large iron skillet to sauté over low to medium heat. Turn each piece of bread frequently until they are lightly browned on each side. Promptly remove them from the skillet when ready, placing on a platter in preparation to add the other ingredients.

Using the entire 4 ounce package of mild goat cheese, evenly distribute the goat cheese on each slice of French bread, and then add 1 tea spoon fig spread to each French bread. Remove the stems from the mission figs and cut each fig in half; place the halved figs on top of the fig spread on each of the French bread. Garnish Fig Delight with mint leaves and serve with Winehaven's Gewürztraminer or Riesling to jump start your palette or if you choose to make it your final course for the evening.

"…extremely tasteful and presented beautifully; Carline's dishes can be enjoyed with all 5 senses and eating at Carline's is a wholesome experience."
Noémie – Paris, France

First or Second Course

Mussels in White Wine Sauce

Whitefish Soup

Thai Crab Cakes

Grainy Mustard Scallops

Gravlax

Mussels in White Wine Sauce

Prepare just before serving
Serves: 4 for a meal or 6-8 as a first course

Ingredients

3 Pounds black mussels
3 Cups Winehaven
     Lakeside Chardonnay
3 Table spoons unsalted butter
3 Table spoons extra virgin olive oil
2 Table spoons ground sea salt
1 Table spoon ground black pepper
1 ½ Cup chopped grape red tomatoes
1 Cup chopped shallots
1 Clove chopped garlic
1 Cup chopped Italian parsley

Ensure the mussels are clean by scrubbing with a brush under running water; place in large bowl and set off to the side. Once all other ingredients are chopped and ready to be combined, in a large stock pot or oversized skillet with lid heat 3 table spoons extra virgin olive oil and 3 table spoons unsalted butter.

Add 1 cup chopped shallots and cook for 5 minutes; add 1 clove chopped garlic and cook for an additional 3 minutes. Next, add remaining ingredients: 1 ½ cup chopped grape red tomatoes; 1 cup chopped Italian parsley; 2 table spoons ground sea salt; 1 table spoon ground black pepper and 3 cups Winehaven's Lakeside Chardonnay. Bring to a vigorous boil and add the 3 pounds of mussels. Stir well, cover the pot or skillet and cook over medium heat for not more than 10 minutes or until all the mussels are opened.

When the mussels are open, directly transfer equal amounts of mussels and sauce to each serving bowl. Garnish with a wedge of toasted and lightly buttered French bread. Extra French bread should be in waiting to consume this lovely sauce making sure to take sips of Winehaven's Lakeside Chardonnay in between.

"Oh my God; this book should have a sound feature button to hear sounds of delight with every mouth full; yum!"
Karen – Tucson, AZ

Whitefish Soup

Prepare and serve the day of or freeze,
unthaw, slowly heat up; serve and enjoy
Serves: 6

Ingredients

2 Packages Blocked Cod Fish
18 Small New Red Potatoes
18 Large pre-cooked Shrimp ready to eat
6 Cups skim milk
1 Large white onion
1 Clove garlic

1 Bunch scallions
4 Table spoons olive oil
¾ Ounce fresh dill
¾ Ounce fresh chive
¾ Cup heavy whipping cream
1½ Teaspoon steak seasoning
Salt to taste

Peel potatoes, dice each potato into small square chunks. Place diced potatoes into a large soup pot, fill with water and bring to a boil cooking potatoes until they are nearly cooked through. Remove from heat and drain off liquid. In large steak pan place the blocks of cod fish, add 4 table spoons olive oil and ½ tea spoon steak seasoning.

On medium heat sauté and break up fish into chunks. When the fish is heated all the way through, remove from heat source and add all contents to large soup pot containing cooked potatoes. Peel the scallions, onion and garlic.

Chop the scallions, onion, garlic, fresh dill, and fresh chives. Save two pinches each of the fresh dill and chives to later garnish the soup. Add all chopped ingredients to the soup pot and the remaining 1 tea spoon steak seasoning. In a glass measuring cup add 2 cups of skim milk and heat in microwave for 6-8 minutes until warm, then add to soup pot. Turn stove on to medium heat setting; continue to heat the other 2 cups each, skim milk in the microwave and add to the soup pot, stirring the soup frequently until it comes to a slight boil.

As the soup begins to bubble at the surface add ¾ cup heavy whipping cream, continuing to stir, bringing the soup to a slight boil. Add salt to taste and reduce heat to low setting. For an additional 5 minutes continue to stir to maintain smoothness and to avoid scalding of the soup.

The soup is now ready to be served. In medium size soup bowl add 1 cup of the soup to each soup bowl. Garnish with 3 each large shrimp, dill and chives. Serve up with your favorite bread and Winehaven's Lakeside Chardonnay. Prepare to let your senses soar!

"International Fare with Home Cooking Comfort"
Diane – Minneapolis, MN

"If a delightfully exquisite experience for your palette is what you crave then Carline's kitchen is where you need to be."
Dawn – Maple Grove

THAI CRAB CAKES

Prepare the day of; makes 6 medium size crab cakes
Serves: 3 -6

INGREDIENTS

3 Packages, 6 ounces each fresh crab meat
2 Packages, 6 ounces each baby spinach
¾ Cup finely chopped parsley
1 Large egg
1 Table spoon minced garlic
1/3 Cup flour
Pinch of salt, black pepper and
Thai red pepper
7 Slices of butter ¼ inch thick each slice

In a large bowl place 3 packages crab meat, ¾ cup finely chopped parsley and a 1/3 cup flour; break open and add one large egg, followed by 1 table spoon minced garlic and a pinch each of salt, black pepper and Thai red pepper. Take 2 of the seven slices of butter and quarter them into four pieces for a total of 8 small squares and add to other ingredients already in the large bowl.

Mix all the ingredients together, blending well. To a large iron skillet add the remaining 5 slices of butter. Turn on heat source to medium setting. While the butter is melting, begin to form the crab mixture into medium size cakes. Add each crab cake to the hot butter in the large iron skillet. Turn each crab cake after 45 seconds; wait another 45 seconds and turn each cake again. Each side should be golden brown throughout. Remove skillet from heat source to a cool burner when cakes are ready. In another large skillet add 2 packages spinach; drizzle with extra virgin olive oil.

Under medium setting heat up the skillet and sauté the spinach until just wilted. On a serving plate add one or two crab cakes and top off with sautéed spinach. Simple ingredients come together providing sophisticated taste, ready to enjoy with Winehaven's Riesling.

"*Extremely flavorful; delicately presented cuisine; precise wine pairing with each course.*"
Kelly – Maple Grove, MN

Grainy Mustard Scallops

Prepare the day of
Serves: 6

Ingredients

18 Large sea scallops
5 Table spoons olive oil
2 Table spoons grainy mustard
2 ½ Cups seafood or chicken stock

2/3 Cup heavy whipping cream
18 Ounces fresh spinach
18 Ounces fresh watercress or arugula
Pinch of Salt & black pepper

Prepare the scallops by patting them dry and season with salt and pepper. In large skillet heat 2 ½ table spoons olive oil until hot. Place the 18 scallops in the skillet and sauté not more than 2 minutes, turning frequently until cooked through.

Remember scallops continue to cook after removing from the skillet. Transfer to a platter and cover with foil to keep warm. In the same skillet add 2 table spoons grainy mustard, 2 ½ cups seafood or chicken stock; stir, bringing to a boil over medium to high heat. Reduce the stock by 1/3. Add 2/3 cup heavy whipping cream; stir bringing to a boil over medium to high heat; reduce to your liking then turn heat source to the lowest setting to keep the sauce warm. In another large skillet add the remaining 2 ½ table spoons olive oil, 18 ounces of fresh spinach and 18 ounces fresh watercress or arugula, sautéing until just wilted.

On 6 large serving plates divide the fresh greens, add 3 scallops to each plate; drizzle the grainy mustard sauce over the scallops and around the perimeter of each plate. Serve and pare with Winehaven's crisp Riesling. Enjoy!

Rinse the salmon filets and pat them dry. Place the salmon filets with the skin sides down in a large type glass baking dish. Mix the ½ cup salt and 2 table spoons sugar together and sprinkle evenly over the salmon filets. In the same fashion sprinkle the 1 tea spoon white pepper evenly over the salmon filets, and then add all of the finely chopped dill to the filets. Next lay the filets together with filet side on top of each other. Tightly wrap the salmon filets in clear plastic cling wrap and lay filets back in the glass baking dish; place in the fridge with a weight on top of the filets.

Each day turn the filets and add fresh chopped dill between the salmon filets if desired. The salmon filets are cured or "gravad" ready after two to three days. Be careful not over process the salmon filets. Remove the clear wrapping and scrape away the ingredients including the dill. With a filet knife slice at an angle the cured salmon into thin slices. Gravlax can be served by itself with your favorite salmon sauce and a lemon wedge or how I prefer to serve it pictured here is on streaked French bread topped with creme fraiche, caviar, sprinkles of capers and fresh dill.

Feeling adventurous? Blend in fresh ground horseradish to the creme fraiche. Pair the lax with Winehaven's Frontenac Gris which contains tropical fruit notes with a soft palate and long finish.

Gravlax

Prepare 2-3 days before
Serves: 8-10

Ingredients

2 Pieces -
1 ½ to 2 pounds each salmon filets
½ Cup Salt
2 Table spoons sugar
1 Tea spoon white pepper
1 Bundle fresh dill, finely chopped

Carline's dishes are not only fabulous-tasting,
but each one is a unique work of art.
Janet – Stillwater, MN

ABOUT THE WINERY

Nestled in the heart of Minnesota's beautiful Chisago Lakes Region, Winehaven Winery and Vineyard's 50 acre estate is situated between three lakes – Lake Ellen, Green Lake and Lake Martha. The lakes, combined with the area's gentle southerly-sloping hillsides, provide natural protection for the delicate grapevine varieties. As a result, the fruit is able to ripen later in the season and the vines are protected from the north winds during winter storms. The winery's perfect location allows for the growing of grapes that consistently produce award winning wines.

As a family owned winery founded as Chisago County's first estate winery in 1995, Winehaven has raised delicious fruits and prized honey for four generations prior to producing high quality wines of distinct regional character. The honeybee on Winehaven's label represents the Peterson's family heritage and history of producing prized honey.

Each wine is crafted in a style that showcases the distinctive character of Winehaven's vineyard that produces very unique wines from grapes, fruit and honey that are found nowhere else on earth. The winery has received more than 200 awards for wine making excellence at New York and California wine competitions during the past ten years along with two US Patents for development of winter-hardy Chisago and Nokomis grapes.

The winery provides a unique selection of white wines, red wines, fruit and honey wines, as well as reserve wines. All are available for tasting year round upon request.

Welcome! - Välkomen!

FEATURED WINES

From left to right: Dear Garden Red Chisago, Frontenac Gris, Gewürztraminer, La Crescent, Lakeside Chardonnay, Lakeside Red, Raspberry Wine, Riesling, Stinger Mead

WINE INDEX

Dear Garden Red Chisago: A semi-sweet red wine with bright cherry aromas and flavors. This wine is one of a kind from patented Chisago grapes grown on the sloping hillsides of Lake Ellen. **Recent Awards:** Silver Medal - 2012 San Francisco International Wine Competition; Silver Medal - 2011 Int'l Cold Climate Wine Competition (Minnesota); Silver Medal - 2011 Finger Lakes International Wine Competition (New York)

Frontenac Gris: This unique wine is made from the winter-hardy Frontenac Gris grape that was developed by the University of Minnesota. It contains tropical fruit notes with a soft palate and long finish. Try it with light pastas, poultry and fish. **Recent Awards:** Gold Medal - 2013 U.S. National Wine Competition; Gold Medal - 2012 U.S. National Wine Competition

Gewürztraminer: Floral aromas blend with pear and pineapple tones to create a pleasant mix of citrus and spice at the finish. Excellent with Asian cuisine! **Recent Awards:** Bronze Medal - 2009 Finger Lakes International Wine Competition (New York)

La Crescent: Made from the winter-hardy La Crescent grape, this wine delivers delightful fruity aromas and flavors that are true to its Midwestern roots. A crisp, delicious finish makes the La Crescent an excellent choice with seafood. **Recent Awards:** Silver Medal - 2011 San Francisco International Wine Competition; Bronze Medal - 2011 Finger Lakes International Wine Competition (New York)

Lakeside Chardonnay: A pale, golden Chardonnay with profound depth and complexity. The bold aroma of the Chardonnay fruit is accompanied by hints of oak, butter and vanilla. This wine is a superb complement to fish and poultry. **Recent Awards:** Silver Medal - 2013 U.S. National Wine Competition

Lakeside Red: This semi-sweet red wine contains overtones of lush cherry that unfold into currants, ripe berry and complex silky tannins. Excellent with grilled meats, pasta and even pizza!

Raspberry Wine: Loaded with flavor, this wine contains more than one and a half pounds of raspberries per bottle! **Recent Awards:** Bronze Medal - 2012 San Francisco International Wine Competition; Silver Medal - 2011 Int'l Cold Climate Wine Competition (Minnesota); Silver Medal - 2010 Int'l Cold Climate Wine Competition (Minnesota); Bronze Medal - 2010 Finger Lakes International Wine Competition (New York)

Riesling: This medium-dry wine contains abundant peach, pear and floral notes that remain distinct through the soft finish and is a perfect complement to fresh fish and poultry. **Recent Awards:** Bronze Medal - 2013 U.S. National Wine Competition; Gold Medal - 2012 U.S. National Wine Competition

Stinger Mead: A smooth, nicely balanced wine with a crisp, delicious finish that boasts a spectacular perfume of honey which is accompanied by an intriguing array of floral scents. **Recent Awards:** Silver Medal - 2013 U.S. National Wine Competition; Gold Medal: 2012 Finger Lakes International Wine Competition

With sincere thanks for your unwavering support and contributions to making "Carline's Fork & Cork Simply Delish!" a reality.

ACKNOWLEDGEMENTS

Mom
Edna Campbell Alter

Brother
Michael Campbell

Sister
Dawn Holtz

Advisors
Traci Brnasford, Peter Crema, Jr., Thomas Nelson, Rich McCrady, Sr.

Designer
Libby Tschida

Editors
Nina Clark, Aisha Friswold, Dawn Holtz

Foreword
David Fhima

Recipe Photographs
Carline Bengtsson

Additional Photography
KeliComm Headshots

Reviews
Edna Alter, Larry Alter, Kelly Berge, Debbie Bushman, Mike Bushman,
Nina Clark, Ryoko Campbell, Michael Campbell, Sarah Fehr, Patti Harris,
Ray Harris, Dawn Holtz, Matt Holtz, Karen Karlsson, Diane Sannes, Robin
Svendsen, Janet Stormo, Noémie Thomas, Todd Tretsven

Winehaven
Cheri, Kevin, Kyle & Troy Peterson